Erlebnis · Vibrant

BONN

Global Players: Konzernzentrale der Deutschen Post/DHL und UN Tower

Global players: corporate headquarters of Deutsche Post/DHL and UN Tower

Erlebnis · Vibrant

BONN

Mit Texten von Monika Hörig
und Fotos von Friedrich Gier

With texts by Monika Hörig
and photographs by Friedrich Gier

Verlag Beleke

Inhalt

Contents

Herausgeber: Norbert Beleke

Text und Konzeption: Dr. Monika Hörig
Fotos: Friedrich Gier (www.gierfotobonn.eu), Michael Sondermann

Übersetzung: St. Clair Consulting
Lektorat und Projektleitung: Thomas Sliepen
Gesamtherstellung: Verlagsgruppe Beleke
Grafische Gestaltung: Jürgen Mosler

Verlagsgruppe: Verlag Beleke GmbH, Essen, Aachen, Dortmund, Lübeck, Wiesbaden
DAS RATHAUS Verlagsges. mbH, Essen
Max SCHMIDT-RÖMHILD KG - Deutschlands ältestes Verlags- und Druckhaus seit 1579 -
Lübeck, Berlin, Essen, Wiesbaden
HANSISCHES VERLAGSKONTOR GmbH, Lübeck
SCHMIDT-RÖMHILD Verlagsgesellschaft mbH Leipzig, Rostock, Schwerin
Verlag Wendler GmbH, Aachen
ELVIKOM Film-Verlag GmbH, Essen
ntv neue television FILM-TV-PRODUKTION GmbH, Essen
www.beleke.de

ISBN 978-3-8215-0635-7

Altes Bonn, neues Bonn – schönes Bonn

Was hat es nur auf sich mit dieser Stadt? Warum ist sie immer wieder etwas Besonderes in diesem an reizvollen, geschichtsträchtigen, bedeutenden Städten wahrlich nicht armen Land? Wieso gerät sie immer wieder in den Mittelpunkt des Geschehens, mal regional, mal politisch, mal international? Und warum staunen immer wieder die Menschen, die Bonn besuchen, was diese angeblich so kleine Stadt zu bieten hat?

Von wegen klein: Mit rund 320.000 Einwohnern kann Bonn im Mittelfeld deutscher Großstädte mithalten, und was inzwischen mindestens ebenso bedeutend ist: Sie wächst und soll bis 2030 über 350.000 Einwohner haben.

Old and new, always splendid: Bonn

What is the story behind this city? How does it continue to stand out as something special in a country with no shortage of charming, historic and important cities? How does it continually find itself at the heart of current affairs – regional, political and international? Why are those who visit Bonn consistently amazed by what this supposedly small town has to offer?

Small town? Not a bit of it! With a population of some 320,000, Bonn holds a mid-table position in the league of German cities. More significantly, however, Bonn is expanding: by 2030, it is likely to have more than 350,000 inhabitants.

Bonns „Gute Stube“: Das Alte Rathaus am Markt

Bonn's jewel in the crown: the Old Town Hall with marketplace

Sicher haben Vater Rhein und Mutter Natur ihre Hände im Spiel: Sie schwemmten Menschen aus aller Welt in die Gegend, sie boten günstige Stellen für die Flussquerung und die Gründung von Ortschaften an. Die Jahrhunderte formten daraus eine Stadt mit ganz eigener Prägung, in der Römer, Märtyrer, Könige, Kurfürsten, Komponisten und schließlich Politiker ihre Spuren hinterließen.

Die Politik war es, die Bonn ins Rampenlicht rückte und zugleich den Stoff für die zahllosen Zeichen der Herablassung lieferten, die Witze über diese „kleine Stadt in Deutschland" (John le Carré), deren bescheidener Habitus für viele als Bühne für das neuerstandene Selbstgefühl nicht ausreichte.

Und Bonn? Bonn hat sich nach dem Umzug der Regierung geschüttelt, sich besonnen, dass der Rhein immer noch fließt und sich auf den Weg zu neuen Ufern gemacht. Nicht mehr oben in den Nachrichten, aber dafür als deutsche UNO-Stadt ganz vorn auf internationalem Parkett, vor allem wenn es um die Themen geht, die wirklich die Welt bewegen, wie den Klimawandel.

Und so sitzen die Bonnerinnen und Bonner, Rheinländer durch und durch, heute in den Straßencafés und Biergärten, spazieren, joggen, radeln am Rhein entlang, laufen durch die Wälder von Kottenforst und Ennert, flanieren durch die kleinen und größeren Geschäftsstraßen. Sie blicken auf UN Tower und Post Tower und die Enten im See in der Rheinaue, sie bummeln durch die Südstadt, durch Muffendorf und das Bundesviertel – und genießen, was viele noch entdecken müssen: Wie schön es hier ist, wie lebenswert und fröhlich diese Stadt sein kann, wie aufgeschlossen und bunt.

Undoubtedly, Mother Nature and Father Rhine have always had a hand in the region's fortunes: they have drawn people here from all over the world, provided convenient points for river crossings and good locations in which to establish communities. Over the centuries, a city with a unique character evolved in this way; a city on which Romans, martyrs, kings, prince-electors, composers and (most recently) politicians have all left their mark.

It was politics that thrust Bonn into the spotlight – and which provided the ammunition for countless cries of disdain and jokes about what John le Carré called 'A Small Town in Germany', a town whose modest stature was regarded by many as inadequate to stage the emerging national sense of self-belief.

And what of Bonn today? Since the government moved out, the city has taken stock, realised the Rhine is still flowing and moved on to pastures new. It may not make so many headlines, but as the German City of the United Nations, Bonn retains a prominent position on the international stage (especially in issues that really matter to the world, such as climate change).

As for the people of Bonn, Rhinelanders through and through, they now relax in the street cafés and beer gardens, go walking and jogging, cycle along the Rhine, ramble through the woods of the Kottenforst nature reserve or the Ennert hills and saunter down shopping streets large and small. They admire the view of the UN building and the Post Tower (and of the ducks on the pond in the Rheinaue Leisure Park) and they stroll through the Südstadt, Muffendorf and Bundesviertel districts. In short, they enjoy what many people have yet to discover: a city of beauty that is good-humoured, open-minded, colourful and a great place to live.

Rechts: Die Poppelsdorfer Allee führt zum gleichnamigen Schloss

Right: Poppelsdorfer Allee leads to the castle of the same name

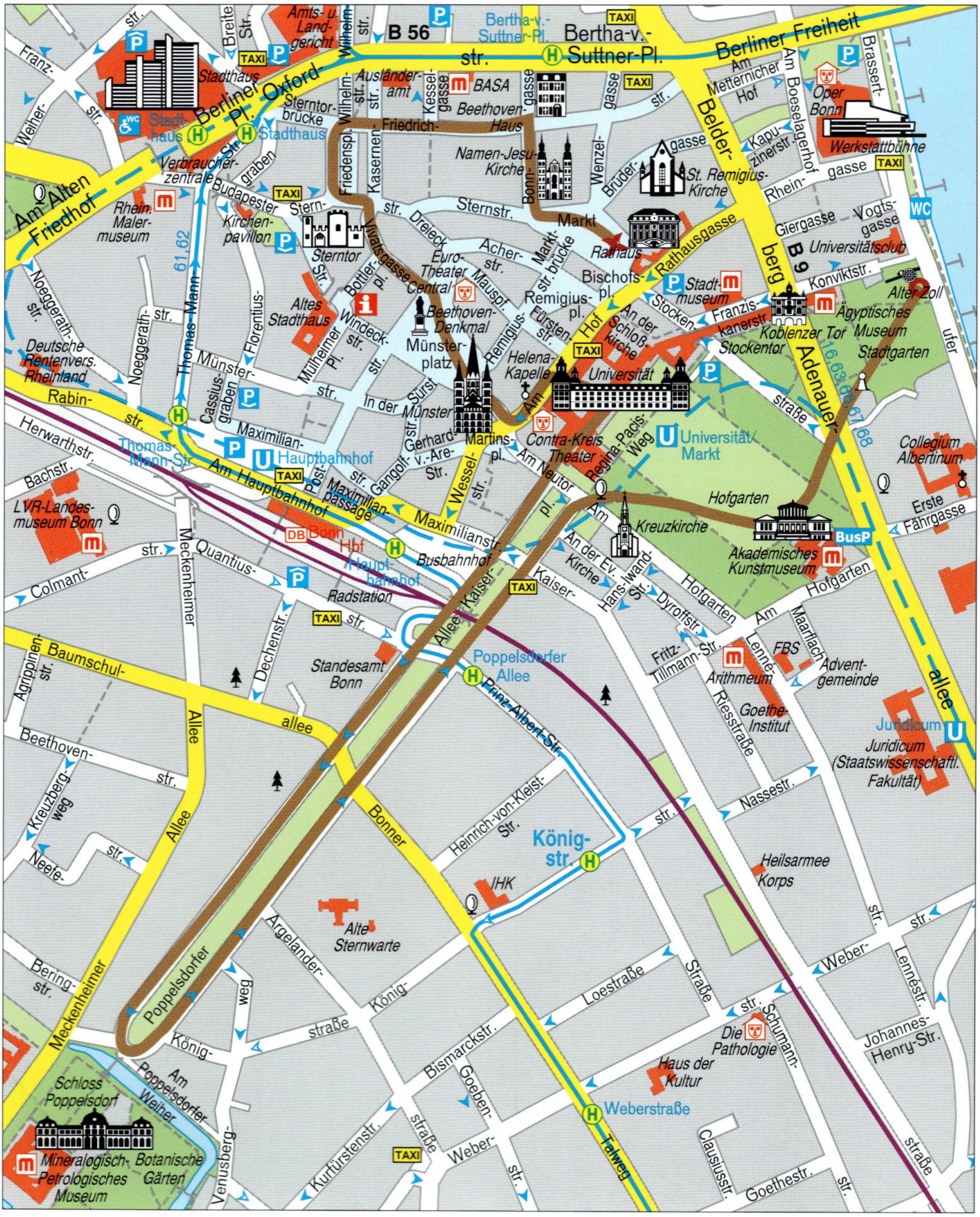

Durch städtische Dichte und viel Grün führt der Rundgang durch die Innenstadt

The urban landscape of the city centre is interspersed with parks and gardens

Durch die Innenstadt

Beginnen wir den Stadtspaziergang am Alten Rathaus, dem zierlichen, in dezentem Rosa und Grau gestrichenen Gebäude am Markt. Kurfürst Clemens August aus dem Hause Wittelsbach legte den Grundstein für den Ort, an dem die Selbstverwaltung der Bürger ihren Anfang nahm. 1738 tagt der Rat zum ersten Mal in dem Rokoko-Bauwerk. Berühmt geworden ist die Freitreppe, auf der zu Bundeshauptstadt-Zeiten gekrönte und ungekrönte Staatsoberhäupter den Bonnerinnen und Bonnern zuwinkten. Hier hielt der erste Präsident der Bundesrepublik Deutschland, Theodor Heuss, 1949 nach seiner Wahl eine Rede. Hier sprachen 1962 Charles de Gaulle und John F. Kennedy zu den Bonnerinnen und Bonnern. Tausende jubelten 1989 vom Marktplatz aus Michail Gorbatschow zu, Nelson Mandela war da und alle Generalsekretäre der

Through the city centre

We start our tour of the city at the old town hall, Altes Rathaus, on the market square. The foundation stone of this gracefully diminutive building, painted in subtle shades of pink and grey, was laid by the Elector Clemens August of the House of Wittelsbach, establishing a seat of self-governance for the citizens. The first session of the council was held in the rococo building in 1738. Its outer staircase became famous during the federal capital era: this is the place from which heads of state, both crowned and uncrowned, waved to the people of Bonn; from which Theodor Heuss, the first President of the Federal Republic of Germany, made his speech following his election in 1949; and from which Charles de Gaulle and John F. Kennedy addressed the citizens of Bonn in 1962. Thousands gathered in Marktplatz to cheer Mikhail

Im Alten Rathaus residiert das Stadtoberhaupt

The mayor's offices are located in the Old Town Hall

Vereinten Nationen von 1975 bis heute. Spiegel dieser bedeutsamen Epoche Bonner Geschichte ist das Goldene Buch der Stadt, in dem sich Monarchen, Staatspräsidenten, Regierungschefs und verdiente Persönlichkeiten, wie zum Beispiel Nobelpreisträger, Künstler und Olympiasieger, verewigt haben.

Über den dreieckigen Platz, auf dem zu jeder Jahreszeit Markt abgehalten wird, geht es zum nahegelegenen Beethoven-Haus. Auf dem Weg zum Geburtshaus des Komponisten lohnt der Blick nach unten: In die Bodenplatten der Bonngasse sind die Porträts berühmter Bonnerinnen und Bonner eingelassen. Und dann steht man – meist gemeinsam mit zahlreichen, oft asiatischen Bewunderern – vor der schmalen, in kräftigem Rosa gehaltenen Fassade mit der hübschen grünen Tür. Im Hinterhaus hat im Dezember 1770 Ludwig van Beethoven das Licht der

Gorbachev in 1989; Nelson Mandela has been here, along with every Secretary General of the United Nations since 1975. The Golden Book of the City of Bonn documents this important era in the history of Bonn by immortalising monarchs, state presidents, heads of government and distinguished personalities including Nobel laureates, artists and Olympic champions.

Crossing the triangular marketplace, which is used for markets all year round, brings us to Beethoven-Haus. On the way to the house in which the composer was born, it's worth keeping your eyes down: portraits of famous sons and daughters of the city are embedded into the paving stones of Bonngasse. We then find ourselves before the narrow, bright pink facade of a building with a charming green door – often in the company of scores of other admirers, many of whom will be from Asia. Ludwig van Beetho-

Jeden Tag ist Markt vor dem Alten Rathaus

Every day is market day in the Old Town Hall square

Welt erblickt. Wir kennen nur seinen Tauftag aus dem Register der Remigiuskirche: 17. Dezember. Sein schmuckloses Geburtszimmer, eine bewegende Sammlung von Musikinstrumenten und Alltagsgegenständen aus seinem Besitz, darunter die immer größer werdenden Hörrohre, die seine zunehmende Schwerhörigkeit ausgleichen sollten – es ist schon ein ganz außergewöhnlicher Ort. Der eigentliche Schatz des Hauses liegt tief darunter im Keller, gesichert mit gepanzerten Türen: die Sammlung von originalen Notenhandschriften. Moderne Technik macht sie im „Digitalen Beethovenhaus" über das Internet weltweit zugänglich. Architektonisches Schmuckstück ist der 1989 eingeweihte Kammermusiksaal im Nebenhaus.

Durch die Einkaufsstraßen, vorbei am Sterntor, einem Rest der Stadtbefestigung, geht der Weg zum Münsterplatz. Er verdankt seinen Namen

ven came into the world in the rear of this building in December 1770. Only the date of his christening is known, from the register of the church of St. Remigius: 17th December. The house itself is an extraordinary place: the austere room in which he was born, the collection of musical instruments and the everyday objects that he owned (including a series of increasingly large ear trumpets designed to compensate for his deteriorating hearing). However, the real treasure of the house is protected by steel doors down in the cellar: the collection of original handwritten sheets of music (thanks to Internet technology, these are now accessible to a global public in the form of Digital Archives). The Chamber Music Hall in the neighbouring building, which opened in 1989, is an architectural gem.

Proceeding through the shopping streets we pass the Sterntor gate, part of the old city forti-

Beethoven-Denkmal auf dem Münsterplatz

Beethoven memorial in Münsterplatz

Damals völlig neuartig: Der dreistöckige Ostchor der Münsterbasilika

Unique at the time: the three-storeyed East Choir of the Münster Basilica der mächtigen, fünftürmigen Basilika, die über der Keimzelle der Stadt steht. Eine „cella memoriae", die ungefähr ins 4. Jahrhundert datiert werden kann und unter der Krypta der heutigen Kirche liegt, scheint der Ursprung gewesen zu sein. Deutlicher wird die Hinwendung zum christlichen Glauben mit der kleinen Kapelle, die im 6. Jahrhundert entstand und 691 erstmals als „Basilica" erwähnt wird. Sie war den Märtyrern Cassius und Florentius aus der legendären Thebäischen Legion geweiht, die im 3. Jahrhundert den Opfertod gestorben sein sollen und bis heute als Bonner Stadtpatrone verehrt werden. Seit wenigen Jahren hat Bonn übrigens auch eine weibliche Schutzheilige: Adelheid, die Äbtissin des Klosters Vilich, deren Stab einem Felsen Wasser, einen kleinen Brunnen („Pützchen"), entlockte.

fications, before arriving at Münsterplatz. The square takes its name from the imposing Bonn Münster, the five-towered basilica that stands over what is thought to have been the actual origin of the city: the cella memoriae below the crypt of the present-day church dates from approximately the fourth century. Firmer evidence of the devotion toward the Christian faith is provided by the small sixth-century chapel which was first documented as a basilica in 691. The chapel was dedicated to Cassius and Florentius of the legendary Theban Legion who, it is believed, were martyred in the third century and remain to this day the patron saints of Bonn. Just a few years ago, Bonn also adopted a female patron saint: Adelaide, the abbess of Vilich Abbey, whose crosier drew a small fountain (a 'Pützchen') from the rocky earth.

Ein Ort der Stille: Der Kreuzgang des Münsters

A place of tranquility: the cloistered courtyard of the Münster

Das Sterntor, ein Überbleibsel der alten Stadtbefestigung

Sterntor, a remnant of the old fortification

Wieder sind es nur wenige Schritte zur nächsten Bonner Sehenswürdigkeit: dem kaisergelb gestrichenen Stadtschloss. Das wunderbare Zeugnis der kurfürstlichen Epoche in Bonn ist heute Hauptsitz der Rheinischen Friedrich-Wilhelms-Universität. Das Gebäude entstand ab 1697 nach Art eines italienischen Palazzo als Vier-Flügel-Bau mit mächtigen, gedrungenen Ecktürmen. Unter Clemens August I. machte es als Schauplatz rauschender Feste von sich reden, zu deren Gästen auch Giacomo Casanova gehörte. Im Inneren bestimmt heute der Alltag einer großen Universität den Rhythmus, kurfürstliche Atmosphäre vermitteln die kleine Schlosskirche und die langgestreckte Fassade zum Hofgarten hin, mit der Figur der „Regina Pacis" über dem Mittelteil und dem barocken Koblenzer Tor.

Das Schloss ist eingebettet in viel Grün: Die Poppelsdorfer Allee, einen Kilometer lang und einst

The next point of interest is once again just a short walk away: the Kurfürstliches Schloss, painted in rich yellow. This exquisite testament to the city's electoral college days now serves as the main building of the University of Bonn. The four-winged castle with the powerfully squat corner towers was constructed in the style of an Italian palazzo in 1697. Under Clemens August I, the castle became a much talked-about stage for glittering parties attended by the likes of Giacomo Casanova. These days the interior moves to the daily rhythm of a major university, but the imperial air lingers in the small castle church, the elongated facade facing onto the Hofgarten park, with the statue of Regina Pacis above the entrance of the central wing and the baroque Koblenz Gate.

The castle is set in expansive grounds. The kilometre-long Poppelsdorfer Allee was originally

Fast 30.000 Studierende bevölkern Bonn und seine Universität

Almost 30,000 students are enrolled at Bonn University

als Kanal zum Poppelsdorfer Schloss gedacht, führt zur Jagdresidenz der Kurfürsten. Zu beiden Seiten der Kastanienallee stehen dicht an dicht die Reihenhäuser der Gründerzeit, eines schöner als das andere, alle sorgfältig renoviert – eine der begehrtesten Wohnadressen der Stadt. Hinter dem Poppelsdorfer Schloss breiten sich die Botanischen Gärten der Universität aus, eine Oase der Ruhe mit immer wieder spannenden Entdeckungen aus der Natur. Hier ist man schon mitten im Universitätsviertel, Studierende aus aller Welt streben in Institute, Labore, Hörsaalgebäude oder sitzen plaudernd auf den Stufen.

Auf der großen Hofgartenwiese, abgeschirmt durch den Gebäuderiegel des Schlosses und durch dichte Baumreihen, finden Jung und Alt gleichermaßen ihre Spielwiese, oft im wörtlichen Sinn. Ihr südliches Ende markiert das neoklassizistische Akademische Kunstmuseum,

planned as a canal and leads to Poppelsdorf Palace, the hunting lodge of the prince-electors. Tightly packed terraces of Gründerzeit-era mansions, lovingly restored and each more magnificent than the last, run down both sides of the chestnut tree-lined avenue, one of the city's most desirable residential streets. Radiating from the rear of Poppelsdorf Palace are the university's Botanic Gardens, an oasis of tranquillity filled with the wonders of nature. This is the heart of the city's university quarter, where students from all corners of the globe sit and chat on the steps when not hard at work in their institutes, laboratories and lecture halls.

The spacious Hofgarten park, watched over and enclosed by the castle buildings and dense rows of trees, provides a playground (often literally) for people of all ages. The southern end of the park is marked by the neo-classical Akademi-

Was kostet die Welt: Uni-Absolventen vor dem Schloss

The world is their oyster: university students celebrating in the castle grounds

Am Koblenzer Tor wacht der Heilige Michael

St. Michael keeping watch at Koblenzer Tor

Neueste Forschungen in ehrwürdigen Mauern: Kekulé-Denkmal vor dem Geographischen Institut der Universität

Cutting-edge research behind ancient walls: Kekulé memorial in front of the Geographic Institute of the university einst Pathologie und heute eine der größten Sammlungen von Gipsabgüssen antiker Werke in Deutschland.

Und nun hinunter zum Rhein. In seiner ganzen Schönheit ist Bonns privilegierte Lage am großen Fluss vom Alten Zoll aus zu sehen. Wilhelm von Humboldt soll den Blick auf den Strom und hinüber zum Siebengebirge als das „Achte Weltwunder" gepriesen haben. Vielleicht ein bisschen pathetisch, aber schön ist's doch.

sches Kunstmuseum, once a museum of pathology that presently houses one of Germany's largest collections of plaster casts of antique sculptures.

We now continue down to the Rhine. Bonn's privileged position on the banks of the mighty river can be appreciated in all its glory from the old customs house, Alter Zoll. Wilhelm von Humboldt is said to have hailed the view of the Rhine and the Siebengebirge hills beyond as the "eighth wonder of the world"; this may be overstating the case somewhat, but there's no denying its beauty.

Der Hofgarten vor dem Akademischen Kunstmuseum

The Hofgarten in front of the Academic Museum of Art

Einst Stadtschloss der Kurfürsten, heute Sitz der Universität

Once city palace of the Electoral Princes, today the seat of the university

Zwischen Stadtschloss und Lustschloss: Die Poppelsdorfer Allee

Situated between the City Palace and the Summer Residence: Poppelsdorfer Allee

Das Stadthaus ist Sitz der Stadtverwaltung

The Town Hall is the seat of the city's administrative bodies

Nur kniend zu erklimmen: Balthasar Neumanns Heilige Stiege in der Kreuzbergkirche

To be climbed on bent knees: the Holy Steps in the Kreuzbergkirche designed by Balthasar Neumann

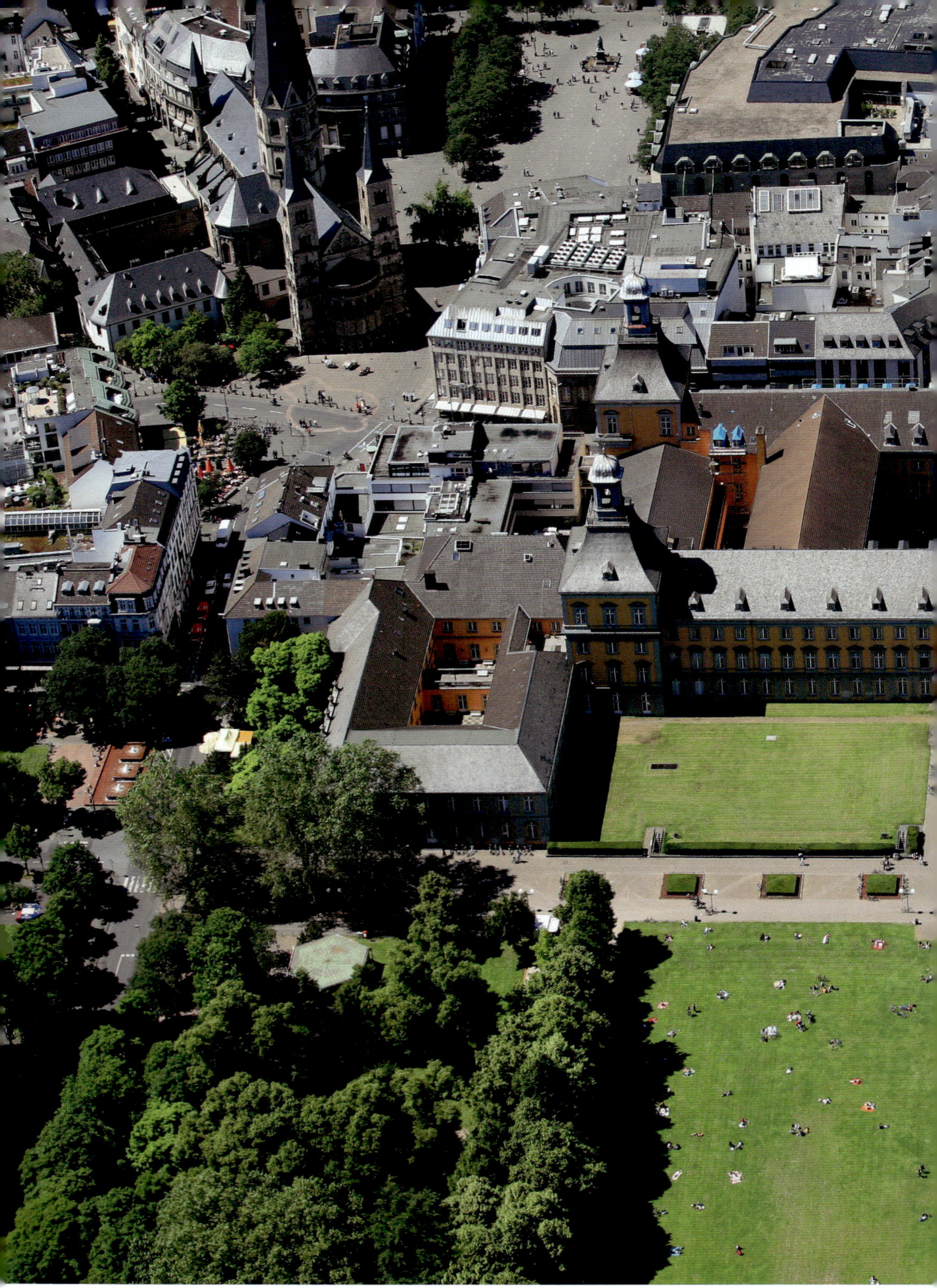

Grüne Insel in der Innenstadt: Der Hofgarten

An island of green in the inner city: the Hofgarten

Einkaufen mit Stil: die Kaiserpassage

Stylish shopping in Kaiserpassage

Bummeln und Genießen in der Friedrichstraße

Window-shopping and enjoying the atmosphere in Friedrichstraße

Die Sternstraße ist seit dem Mittelalter Geschäftsstraße

Sternstraße was first established for trading purposes during the Middle Ages

Auf dem Kaiserplatz

Kaiserplatz

Schlendern und Shoppen in Bonns weitläufiger Fußgängerzone

Taking a stroll and shopping in Bonn's extensive pedestrian zone

„Am Dreieck" ist es gemütlich

Perfect place for a rest: "Am Dreieck"

Das World Conference Center Bonn

The World Conference Centre Bonn

Fassaden in der Südstadt

Facades in the south of the city

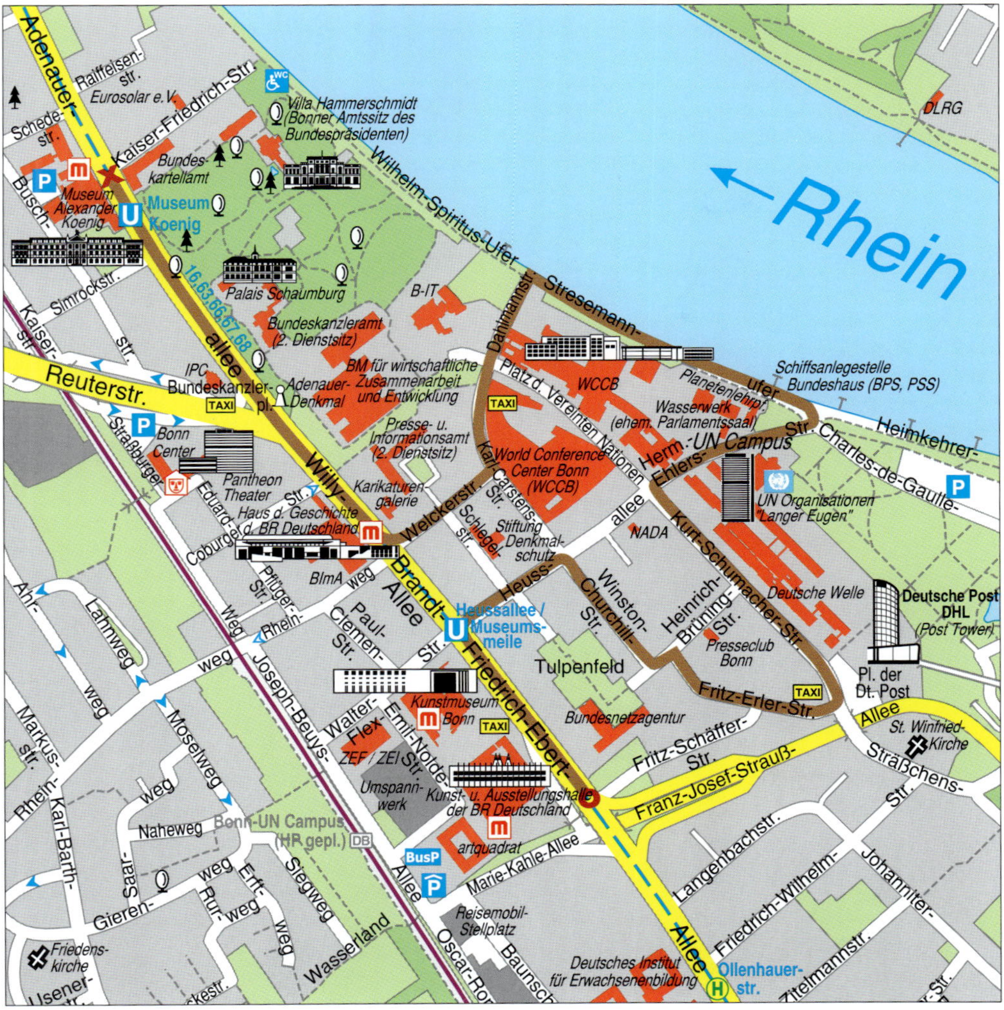

Villa Hammerschmidt und UN Tower: Beim Rundgang durch das Bundesviertel wird Bonns Vergangenheit und sein heutiges Profil deutlich

Villa Hammerschmidt and UN Tower: a walk through the government quarter provides a good insight into Bonn – past and present

Im Bundesviertel

Die Adenauerallee führt direkt ins Herz der jüngeren Geschichte Bonns. Erste Station ist das Museum Alexander Koenig, dessen Schausammlung das Leben auf unserem „blauen Planeten“ dokumentiert. Hier trat 1948 der Parlamentarische Rat zu seiner konstituierenden Sitzung zusammen: Die Geburtsstunde der deutschen Demokratie nach dem Zweiten Weltkrieg. Auf der anderen Straßenseite steht das Palais

The Bundesviertel

Adenauerallee provides a direct route into the more recent history of Bonn. The first stop is the Museum Alexander Koenig, whose exhibition charts life on our blue planet. The museum was the venue for the rebirth of German democracy after the Second World War when the Parliamentary Council held its constitutional convention here in 1948. On the far side of the street is Palais Schaumburg, once the royal residence of

Naturkundemuseum und Ort der deutschen Geschichte: Museum Alexander Koenig

Museum of Natural Science and place of history: Museum Alexander Koenig

Von der Villa zum Bundeskanzleramt: Das Palais Schaumburg

From villa to Federal Chancellery: Palais Schaumburg

Schaumburg, einst Adelspalais der unglücklichen Preußen-Prinzessin Viktoria, die einen Abenteurer heiratete und verarmt starb. In den Räumen des Palais' residierte der erste Bundeskanzler der Nachkriegszeit, Konrad Adenauer. Sein Büro samt verschrammter Aktentasche ist heute noch zu besichtigen. Das Teehaus im Park ist wieder zugänglich.

Nur einen Steinwurf vom Palais Schaumburg entfernt die Villa Hammerschmidt, Bonner Amtssitz des Bundespräsidenten bis heute. Das Staatsoberhaupt hält sich nicht selten zu Gesprächen und Empfängen am Rhein auf, und zu besonderen Terminen wird hier getraut. Dann das einstige Bundeskanzleramt, heute Sitz des Ministeriums für wirtschaftliche Zusammenarbeit und Entwicklung. Der Kanzlerbungalow mit seinen winzigen Zimmern ist renoviert und steht bei Führungen und Konzerten offen.

Ab hier führt der Spaziergang durch die Zeugnisse deutscher Geschichte die Wandlung

the unfortunate Princess Victoria of Prussia who married an adventurer and died in poverty. Konrad Adenauer, the first Federal Chancellor of the postwar era, also resided in the palace. It is possible to visit his office, complete with battered briefcase, and the teahouse in the park is also open again.

A stone's throw from Palais Schaumburg is Villa Hammerschmidt, official residence of the Federal President to this day. The head of state frequently stays here while hosting meetings and receptions by the Rhine; the villa is also used for weddings on special occasions. The former Federal Chancellery building today accommodates the Federal Ministry for Economic Cooperation and Development. Meanwhile the renovated Chancellor's Bungalow, with its tiny rooms, is open for guided tours and concerts.

From this point, the transformation of Bonn over the past 15 or 20 years unfurls before our eyes in the form of testimonials to German history.

Das Adenauerdenkmal nahe dem Palais Schaumburg, dem Dienstsitz des ersten Bundeskanzlers

Adenauer memorial near Palais Schaumburg, official residence of Germany's first Chancellor

Der Bonner Amtssitz des Bundespräsidenten: Die Villa Hammerschmidt

The official Bonn residence of the German President: Villa Hammerschmidt

Internationales Parkett: Tagen im Hotel Maritim

International flair: conferences at Hotel Maritim

Bonns in den letzten 15, 20 Jahren vor Augen. Unmittelbar am Rhein liegt der einstige Plenarsaal des Deutschen Bundestages. Das lichtdurchflutete Gebäude von Behnisch und Partner wurde 1992 eingeweiht, da war der Beschluss, einen Teil der Ministerien nach Berlin zu verlagern, schon gefallen. In den blauen Sesseln beraten heute Tagungsteilnehmer aus aller Welt, sitzen Firmenvertreter bei Präsentationen oder Aktionäre bei Hauptversammlungen. Rechts und links des Plenarsaales erstrecken sich die weißen Gebäuderiegel der früheren Bundestagsverwaltung im strengen Bauhausstil. Die heutigen Türschilder weisen internationale Einrichtungen aus, links ein paar kleinere, rechts demnächst das UNO-Klimasekretariat (UNFCCC).

Die Vereinten Nationen in Bonn? Ja, das zweite politische Zentrum des Landes hat sich seit 1996 zur deutschen UNO-Stadt entwickelt. Vom 19-stöckigen Hochhaus, dem „Langen Eugen", der zu Bundeshauptstadt-Zeiten die Büros der

The one-time plenary chamber of the German Bundestag, close to the river, is a light-filled structure built by Behnisch & Partner and inaugurated in 1992 – by which time the decision to relocate a number of ministries to Berlin had already been made. Today, the blue seats are occupied by conference participants from around the world, company representatives attending presentations or shareholders taking part in annual general meetings. The plenary chamber is flanked on either side by the austerely white Bauhaus buildings of the former Bundestag complex, but today the names above the doors are those of international establishments: smaller institutions line up to the left, while the Secretariat of the United Nations Framework Convention on Climate Change (UNFCCC) is located to the right.

What of the United Nations in Bonn? The country's second political centre did indeed emerge as the German City of the United Nations in 1996. The 19-floor high rise known as Langer

Herausragende Architektur: Der Post Tower

Outstanding architecture: the Post Tower

Wo alles begann: Seit 1996 weht die blaue UNO-Flagge am Haus Carstanjen

Where it all began: the blue flag of the United Nations has been flying at Haus Carstanjen since 1996

Abgeordneten beherbergte, grüßt das blau-weiße Symbol der Vereinten Nationen.

Fast 20 Organisationen haben sich hier angesiedelt. Sie alle arbeiten für das derzeit wichtigste Thema, das unsere Welt bewegt: Nachhaltigkeit. Wie machen wir die Welt widerstandsfähig gegen die extensive Nutzung, der die Ressourcen seit Jahrzehnten ausgesetzt sind? Wie schützen wir das Klima, verhindern die Ausbreitung der Wüsten, wie erhalten wir aussterbende Tierarten, und wie lassen sich Naturereignisse vorhersagen, die in Katastrophen für zahllose Menschen münden?

Zu Füßen des UN Towers erstreckt sich das Funkhaus der Deutschen Welle, des deutschen Auslandssenders, der seine Programme in 30 Sprachen in alle Welt ausstrahlt. Direkt daneben erhebt sich das Symbol des neuen Bonns, die

Eugen, which accommodated the offices of members of parliament when Bonn was the federal capital, now stands as the blue and white symbol of the United Nations.

The building provides a base for 20 organizations involved in the number one issue currently facing the world: sustainability. How can we ensure the world withstands the pressure on resources that has been so high for many decades? How can we safeguard the climate, halt the encroaching deserts, protect endangered species and predict natural events that lead to disaster for countless people?

The broadcasting centre of Deutsche Welle, Germany's international broadcaster whose programmes are transmitted around the globe in 30 languages, sits at the feet of the UN Tower. Alongside is the soaring, elliptical symbol of the

Die Lichttürme sind das Markenzeichnen der Kunst- und Ausstellungshalle der Bundesrepublik Deutschland

The towers of light are the hallmark of Germany's Art and Exhibition Centre

Konzernzentrale der Deutschen Post/DHL, mit ihren schlanken 162 Metern höher als der Kölner Dom. Der „Mercurius“ von Markus Lüpertz vor seiner Tür ist ein fast nostalgischer Hinweis auf die Wurzeln eines der größten Logistik-Konzerne der Welt.

Auch die Museumsmeile gehört zu diesem Viertel. Wie Perlen auf einer Schnur folgt hier ein spektakuläres Haus auf das andere. Die Reihe beginnt mit dem schon erwähnten Museum Koenig. Es folgt das Haus der Geschichte der Bundesrepublik Deutschland, das einen spannenden Rundgang durch die Jahrzehnte bundesrepublikanischer Vergangenheit ermöglicht. Dann das Kunstmuseum Bonn. Der lichte Bau mit seinem großen Segeldach beherbergt eine reizvolle Sammlung von Werken August Mackes, der einige Jahre in Bonn gearbeitet hat, und der Rheinischen Expressionisten, dazu dokumentiert es deutsche Kunst nach 1945. In der benachbarten Kunst- und Ausstellungshalle der Bundesrepublik Deutschland geben sich die bedeutenden Museen der Welt von Zeit zu Zeit die Ehre, locken große Retrospektiven und faszinierende Werkschauen Hunderttausende an. Die drei Lichttürme auf dem begehbaren Dach sind zum Markenzeichen geworden.

new Bonn: the headquarters of Deutsche Post/DHL, at 162 metres taller than Cologne Cathedral. Mercurius, the statue created by Markus Lüpertz at the entrance of the building, is an almost nostalgic indication of the roots of one of the world's biggest logistics groups.

This part of Bonn is also home to the city's Museum Mile, where one spectacular collection links up with another like a string of pearls. The series starts with the aforementioned Museum Koenig and moves on to the Haus der Geschichte, which chronicles the history of the Federal Republic of Germany. An absorbing retrospective of Germany's recent decades is followed by the Kunstmuseum Bonn, a bright construction with a roof resembling a giant sail. The Kunstmuseum holds appealing collections of works by August Macke, who was active in Bonn for several years, as well as the Rhenish Expressionists; at the same time, it documents German art since 1945. Next door is the Art and Exhibition Hall of the Federal Republic of Germany, which proudly hosts artefacts from the world's foremost museums; its major retrospectives and fascinating exhibitions attract visitors in their hundreds of thousands. The three towers of light on the roof, which is accessible to visitors, have become the building's landmark.

Eine Plastik von Henry Moore vor dem Bundesministerium für wirtschaftliche Zusammenarbeit und Entwicklung, einst Bundeskanzleramt

A sculpture by Henry Moore, outside the Federal Ministry for Economic Cooperation and Development, once home to the Federal Chancellery

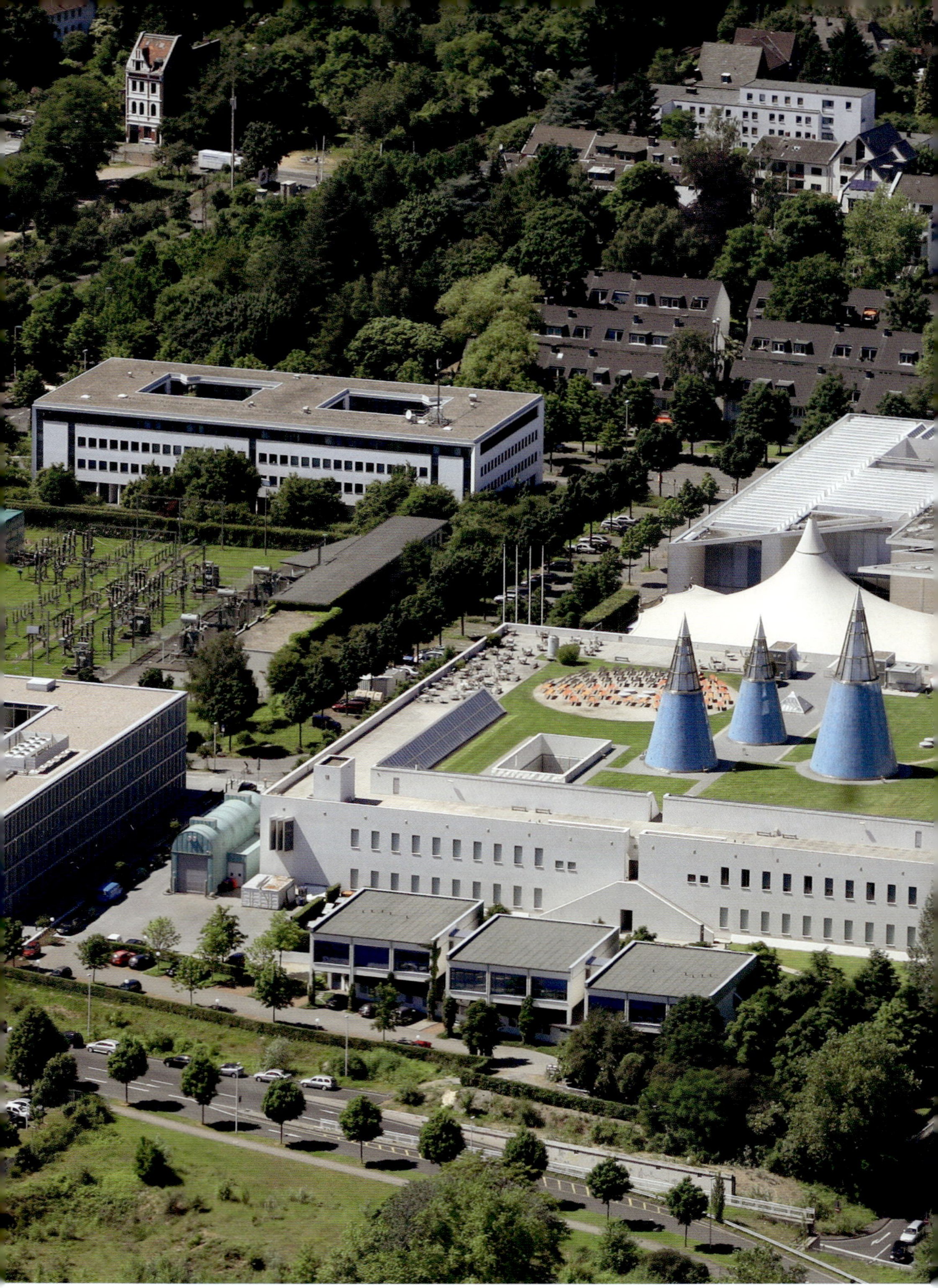

Einzigartiges Ensemble: Die Bonner Museumsmeile

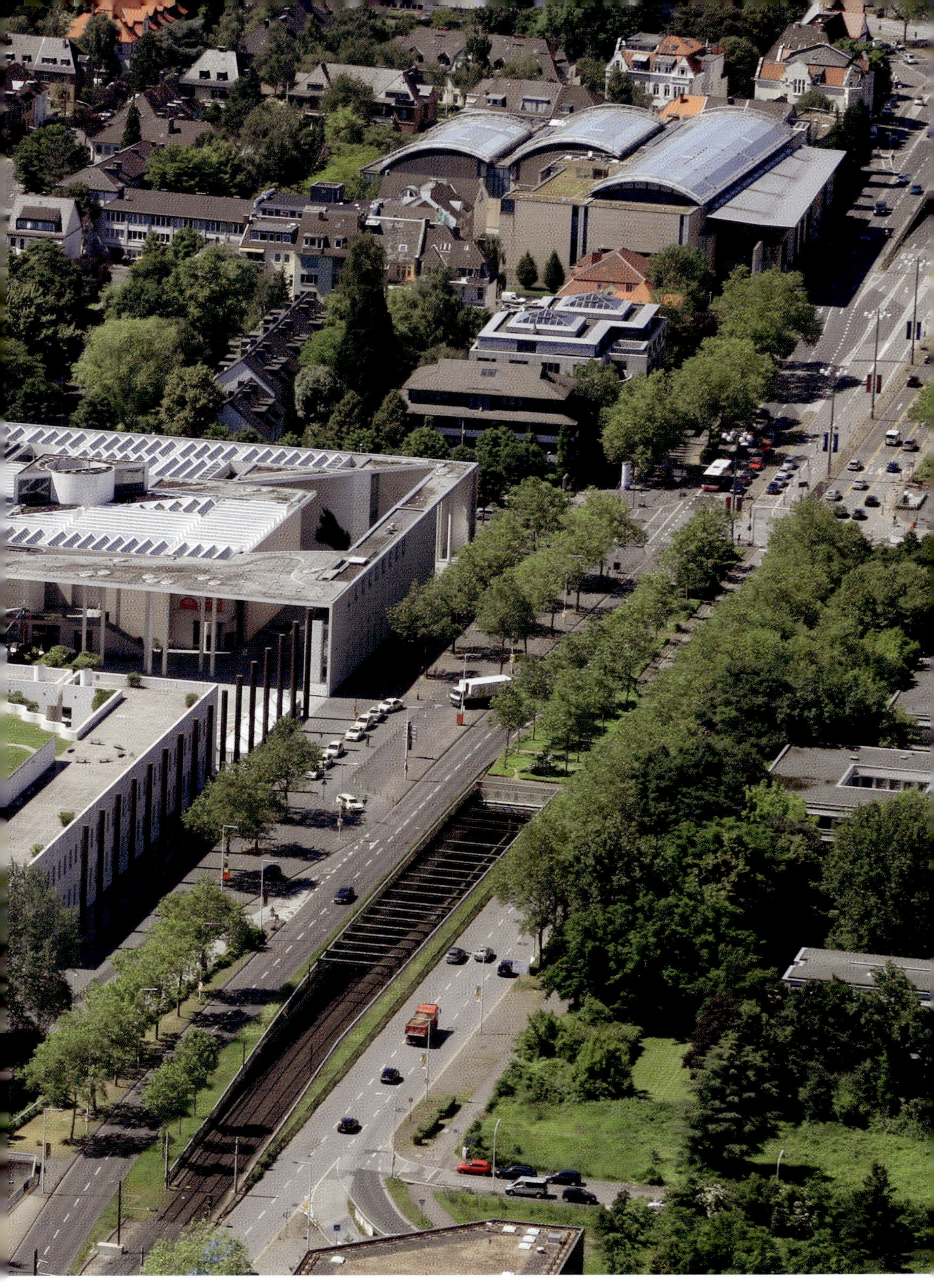

Unique cultural project: the Museum Mile

In der Kunst- und Ausstellungshalle der Bundesrepublik Deutschland

Art and Exhibition Centre of the Federal Republic of Germany

Schauplatz zahlreicher Tagungen: Das Hotel Maritim

Popular place for conferences: Hotel Maritim

Markus Lüpertz' „Mercurius" am Post Tower

Markus Lüpertz's "Mercurius" at the Post Tower

Die alljährlichen Museumsmeilenfeste sind beliebt bei Jung und Alt

The annual festivities of the Museum Mile are very popular with all age groups

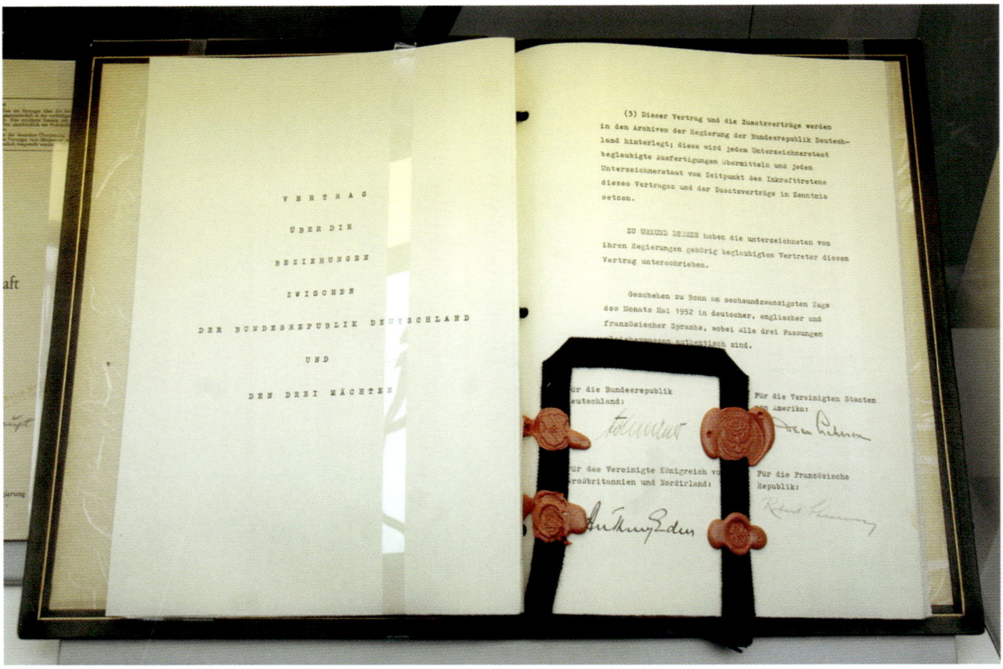

Dokumente der Zeitgeschichte im Haus der Geschichte, hier ein Vertrag von 1954

Historical documents exhibited at Haus der Geschichte: a contract dating back to 1954

Hautnah an der jüngsten Vergangenheit: Das Haus der Geschichte der Bundesrepublik Deutschland

History unfolding: Haus der Geschichte of the Federal Republic of Germany

Für Nostalgiker: Lichtspielhaus im Haus der Geschichte

Bygone era: movie theatre at the Haus der Geschichte

Flower Power: Hippie-Bulli aus Kalifornien im Haus der Geschichte der Bundesrepublik Deutschland

Flower Power: Hippie van from California on display at the Haus der Geschichte

Arbeiten im Grünen: Das Bundesviertel

The Bundesviertel is interspersed with green spaces

Im einstigen Abgeordneten-Hochhaus residiert heute die UNO

The high-rise building once used by members of parliament has become home to the United Nations Organization

Im Wasserwerk trat der Bundestag zusammen, als der neue Plenarsaal gebaut wurde

The Bundestag held conferences in the Wasserwerk while the new plenary assembly room was beeing built

Internationale Experten schätzen Bonn als Tagungsort

Experts from around the globe value Bonn as a venue for conferences

Der afghanische Staatspräsident Karsai trägt sich ins Goldene Buch ein

President of Afghanistan Hamed Karsai signs The Golden Book of the City of Bonn

UNO-Generalsekretär Ban Ki-Moon in Bonn

Secretary-General of the United Nations Ban Ki-Moon on a visit to Bonn

UNO-Generalsekretär Kofi Annan und Bundeskanzlerin Angela Merkel weihen den neuen UN Campus ein

General-Secretary of the United Nations Kofi Annan and Chancellor Angela Merkel at the inauguration ceremony of the new UN Campus

Nelson Mandela auf der Bonner Rathaustreppe

Nelson Mandela on the steps of the Bonn town hall

Hochkarätige Mischung: Ministerien, Unternehmen, Vereinte Nationen

Ivy league: ministries, corporate head offices, United Nations

Auch architektonisch ein Juwel: Das städtische Kunstmuseum

Also an architectural jewel: the Bonn Museum of Art

Das Kunstmuseum der Stadt Bonn

The Bonn Museum of Art

Katharina Grosses „In Seven Days Time“ ist der neue Blickfang am Kunstmuseum Bonn

"In Seven Days' Time" by Katharina Grosse is the new focal point of the Bonn Museum of Art

Der Firmensitz der T-Mobile in Bonn-Beuel

Company HQ of T-Mobile in Bonn-Beuel

High Tech in Sachen Kommunikation:
Das Forum von T-Mobile

High-tech communications:
the T-Mobile Forum

Bundespräsident Köhler mit Biodiversitätsexperten aus aller Welt

President Horst Köhler at a meeting with internationally renowned biodiversity experts

Bundeskanzlerin Merkel im früheren Plenarsaal

Chancellor Angela Merkel in the former plenary assembly room

Post Tower und UN Tower beherrschen heute das Bundesviertel

The Post Tower and the UN Tower dominate the Bundesviertel

Ein Bild geht um die Welt: Gorbatschow 1989 in Bonn

Of international interest: Gorbachev's visit to Bonn in 1989

Bundespräsident Wulff und Bonns Oberbürgermeister Nimptsch

President Christian Wulff and Mayor of Bonn Jürgen Nimptsch

Am Rhein entlang

Von seiner schönsten Seite zeigt sich Bonn am Rhein. Wer gut zu Fuß ist, beginnt linksrheinisch gleich in der Innenstadt, etwas nördlich der Kennedybrücke, an der Beethovenhalle. Sie ist das dritte Bauwerk dieses Namens und wurde 1959 eingeweiht. Unter ihrem kupfergedeckten Kuppeldach wurde mit der Wahl mehrerer Bundespräsidenten Geschichte geschrieben. Vor allem aber hat hier die Pflege des musikalischen Erbes der Stadt seinen Platz, mit dem Beethoven-Orchester Bonn an der Spitze und den jährlichen Beethovenfesten als Höhepunkt. Dass zurzeit über eine neue Philharmonie diskutiert wird, tut der historischen Rolle der in die Jahre gekommenen Multifunktionshalle keinen Abbruch.

Weiter geht es Richtung Süden, vorbei an der 1965 gebauten Oper mit ihrer charakteristischen Schuppenfassade, am Wohnhaus des

Along the Rhine

It is the Rhine that gives Bonn its fullest beauty. Those who enjoy walking should start from central Bonn (on the left bank of the Rhine), just to the north of Kennedy Bridge. Officially opened in 1959, the present Beethovenhalle is the third structure to bear the name. History has been made beneath its copper-plated dome roof with the election of several Federal Presidents. However, the main purpose of the building is to uphold the city's musical heritage through the twin pillars of the Beethoven Orchestra and the annual Beethovenfest programme. Current discussions over a new philharmonic hall in no way diminish the historic status of the multi-purpose hall, which is simply showing its age.

Continuing south, we pass the imbricated facade of the opera house (built in 1965), the residence of the scholar and revolutionary Ernst

Am Rheinufer vor der Villa Hammerschmidt

The banks of the river Rhine in front of Villa Hammerschmidt

Oase der Stille: Der Japanische Garten in der Rheinaue

Oasis of tranquility: Japanese Gardens in the Rheinaue Leisure Park

Gelehrten und Revolutionärs Ernst Moritz Arndt, einem Juwel des Biedermeiers, an einstigen Ministeriumsgebäuden, in denen heute zum Beispiel der Bundesrechnungshof sitzt, an großen Villen und bis zum ehemaligen Bundestag, der gerade von der Rheinseite aus Sinnbild der maßvollen Bonner Demokratie ist.

Und schon wartet die nächste Attraktion auf den Besucher, der jetzt allerdings besser ein Fahrrad gebrauchen könnte: Die Rheinaue, das riesige Freizeitgelände Bonns, das Gelände der Bundesgartenschau 1969. Ob Japanischer oder Duftgarten, ob Große Blumenwiese oder Schiffchensee – die Bonnerinnen und Bonner tummeln sich hier zu jeder Jahreszeit.

Von der Konrad-Adenauer-Brücke aus blickt man auf den „Bonner Bogen" im Süden Beuels. Diese alte Industriebrache hat sich zu einem Standort hochspezialisierter Unternehmen gewandelt. Die denkmalgeschützten Teile der einstigen Zementfabrik sind in moderne Architektur

Moritz Arndt (a Biedermeier-period masterpiece), former government buildings (now housing the Federal Court of Auditors, amongst other institutions) and some sizeable mansions before arriving at the former Bundestag, the emblem of democracy in Bonn that appears particularly modest from its Rhine-facing side.

The next attraction is already awaiting the visitor, although a bicycle would now be useful: the Rheinaue is the city's sprawling leisure park and the site of the Federal Horticultural Show in 1969. The people of Bonn flock here at any time of year: to the Japanese garden, the scented garden, the spreading 'field of flowers' and the Schiffchensee lake.

The Konrad-Adenauer Bridge overlooks the Bonner Bogen development in the southern part of the Beuel district, a former industrial brownfield site now transformed into a base for some highly specialised businesses. Heritage-protected sections of a one-time cement works have been in-

integriert, mittendrin steht ein futuristisch anmutendes Hotel.

Am südlichen Rand der Rheinaue steht mit der Amerikanischen Siedlung und ihrer im Südstaaten-Stil erbauten kleinen Kirche eine Erinnerung an Bundeshauptstadtzeiten. Mit dem Forschungszentrum CAESAR (Center for Advanced European Studies and Research) und mit Haus Carstanjen, einem Schlösschen mit angebautem Bürotrakt, in dem bis 2012 das Klimasekretariat der Vereinten Nationen seinen Sitz hat, trifft man auf Beispiele für Bonns Strukturwandel nach dem Umzugsbeschluss: Wissenschaft und Internationale Stadt.

Jetzt ist man schon in Bad Godesberg: Stille, baumgesäumte Straßen mit wunderbaren Villen, einst bevorzugter Sitz der Diplomatie, prägen den Stadtteil. Über ihm wacht seit 1210 die Godesburg, deren Zerstörung 1583 praktisch nur der Turm gut überstanden hat. Am Rande des

tegrated into a modern new complex, at the heart of which stands a futuristic-looking hotel.

At the southern boundary of the Rheinaue park, the Amerikanische Siedlung - an American residential estate with a small church built in the style of the American south - harks back to federal capital days. The CAESAR research facility (Center of Advanced European Studies and Research) and the castle Haus Carstanjen (with its attached wing of offices housing the Secretariat of the United Nations Framework Convention on Climate Change until 2012) are regarded as examples of the structural transformation of Bonn into an international city of science since the government relocated to Berlin.

By now we have reached Bad Godesberg. The former diplomatic quarter is characterised by peaceful streets lined with trees and sumptuous mansions and is guarded by the Godesburg, the castle built in 1210 and destroyed in 1583,

Der UN Tower überragt die Bonner Rheinaue

The UN Tower dominates the Bonner Rheinaue

einladenden Stadtparks steht mit der Redoute ein weiteres Zeugnis der eleganten und unterhaltungsfreudigen Kurfürstenzeit. In ihrem klassizistischen Ambiente soll der junge Ludwig van Beethoven dem großen Joseph Haydn vorgespielt haben.

Zurück geht es über die B 9, die große Magistrale zwischen Bonns Innenstadt und Bad Godesberg. Bürohaus reiht sich an Bürohaus, manches mit bedeutsamer Geschichte wie die frühere Ständige Vertretung der DDR und etliche Botschaften. Die einstige „Diplomatenrennbahn" führt vorbei am Hauptsitz der Deutschen Telekom, einer der „Global Players", der von Bonn aus Geschäfte in aller Welt steuert. Zu beiden Seiten der Straße stehen die Bürohäuser des Branchenriesen, eine elegante Glasbrücke verbindet sie.

leaving little but the tower standing. On the edge of the welcoming Stadtpark is the Redoute ballroom, another monument to the elegantly convivial age of the prince-electors. The young Ludwig van Beethoven is said to have played to the older Joseph Haydn in these classical surroundings.

Heading back via the B9, the main thoroughfare linking the centre of Bonn to Bad Godesberg, we pass one office block after another. Many have interesting histories, having formerly housed embassies and the Permanent Mission of the GDR. This 'diplomatic racetrack' of yesteryear leads to the headquarters of Deutsche Telekom, one of the global players that oversees its worldwide operations from Bonn; the offices of this giant of the sector occupy both sides of the street, connected by a graceful glass bridge.

Erholung am breiten Strom in Oberkassel

Relaxing on the river banks in Oberkassel

29 Kilometer rechts und links des Stromes: Das Rheinufer in Bonn

The banks of the river Rhine in Bonn stretch across 29 kilometres to the left and the right

Am ersten Mai-Samstag steht der „Rhein in Flammen“

The "Rhine in Flames" on the first Saturday in May

Strandgefühl am großen Strom

"Beach culture" on the banks of the great river

Beim Triathlon wird der Rhein zur Sportarena

The Rhine is transformed into a sports arena during the triathlon events

Romanisches Schmuckstück: Doppelkirche Schwarz-Rheindorf

Romanesque jewel: two churches housed in one building in Schwarz-Rheindorf

Alt und neu: Godesburg und Innenstadt von Bad Godesberg

Old meets new: Godesburg and the inner city of Bad Godesberg

Das Wahrzeichen des Kurorts: Die Godesburg

The symbol of the spa: Godesburg

Stilvoll speisen in einer der schönen Villen Bad Godesbergs

Dining in style in one of the beautiful residences in Bad Godesberg

„La Redoute“ in Bad Godesberg, 2011 renoviert, ist Rahmen für Empfänge und Konzerte

"La Redoute" in Bad Godesberg offers a perfect setting for receptions and concerts, refurbished in 2011

Fachwerkromantik des 18./19. Jahrhunderts in Muffendorf

Quaint half-timbered houses in Muffendorf, dating back to the 18th/19th century

Eine alte Rotbuche im Stadtgarten

An old European beech in Stadtgarten

Stöbern auf mehreren Kilometern: Flohmarkt in der Rheinaue

Miles and miles of fun: looking for treasures at the flea market in Rheinaue

So wohnten die Gelehrten der Universität im 19. Jahrhundert: Ernst-Moritz-Arndt-Haus

Scholars' quarters at the university during the 19th century: Ernst-Moritz-Arndt-Haus

Beliebtes Ausflugsziel: Das Weinhäuschen in Mehlem

Popular tourist attraction: Weinhäuschen in Mehlem

Von zeitloser Eleganz: Die Universitätsbibliothek wurde 1960 erbaut

Timeless elegance: the University library was built in 1960

Im Forschungszentrum CAESAR geht es um Neurowissenschaften

The research centre CAESAR specialises in neuroscience

Rund um Bonn

Bonn hält, was es als Tor zum romantischen Rhein verspricht: Unmittelbar vor den südlichen Stadtgrenzen bestimmen Berge und Burgen das Bild. Das Siebengebirge, dessen Name sich von „Siefen" – feuchte Täler – herleitet, verbirgt manch idyllisches Fleckchen zwischen seinen 50 Bergen. Der bekannteste ist der Petersberg mit der dem Heiligen Petrus geweihten barocken Kapelle. Kloster, Gutshof, Kurhotel, Gästehaus der Bundesregierung: Die Geschichte des Anwesens auf seiner Spitze, von dessen Terrasse aus man einen grandiosen Blick auf den Rhein und Bonn hat, ist bunt. Bis heute wissen Staatsoberhäupter und Prominente das nur über eine Serpentinenstraße erreichbare und damit gut abzuschirmende gastliche Refugium zu schätzen.

Der benachbarte Drachenfels gilt als höchster Berg der Niederlande, weil er so viele Besucher aus dem Nachbarland anzieht. Schloss Dra-

Around Bonn

Bonn is the gateway to the romance of the Rhine: at the southern limits of the city, the landscape is immediately one of hills and castles. The 50 peaks of the Siebengebirge hills (taking their name from 'Siefen', a form of ravine) conceal countless idyllic spots. Best known is the Petersberg, with its baroque chapel dedicated to Saint Peter. Monastery, manor house, health resort, accommodation for guests of the Federal Republic of Germany: the estate at the summit of this mountain, where a terrace commands superb views of the Rhine and of Bonn, can look back on a colourful history. The privacy afforded by this splendid refuge, which is accessible only via a winding mountain road, is still valued by heads of state and VIPs alike.

The next peak, the Drachenfels, is sometimes referred to as the highest mountain in the Netherlands because of the many visitors it attracts

Steine der Abteikirche Heisterbach wurden zum Bau der Feste Ehrenbreitstein in Koblenz verwendet

Stones taken from Heisterbach Abbey were used for the construction of Feste Ehrenbreitstein in Koblenz

chenburg scheint mit seinen Türmchen und Erkern einem gründerzeitlichen Märchen entsprungen zu sein. Park mit Drachenhöhe, Naturschutzmuseum und Nibelungenhalle bilden eine eigenwillige Attraktion.

Im Kurort Bad Honnef am Fuße des Drachenfelsens wird noch einmal bundesdeutsche Geschichte lebendig: Das Bundeskanzler-Adenauer-Haus ermöglicht Einblicke in das Leben des ersten deutschen Regierungschefs, Rosengarten inklusive.

Am linken Rheinufer, gleich hinter der südlichen Bonner Stadtgrenze, begegnet der Reisende in Rolandseck einem besonders schönen Stück Rheinlandschaft: Im Strom die Inseln Nonnenwerth und Grafenwerth, an Land der Bahnhof aus der Mitte des 19. Jahrhunderts, der zum Synonym für hochklassige Kultur in kleinem Rahmen geworden ist. Der „Kunstbahnhof" hat erst jüngst mit dem in den Hang gebauten Arp-Museum eine spektakuläre Erweiterung erfahren. Über allem schwebt der Rolandsbogen, letztes Relikt der Burg Rolandseck und beliebtes Reiseziel der Romantiker einst und jetzt.

from the neighbouring country. With its turrets and oriel windows, Schloss Drachenburg is a vision from a Gründerzeit fairytale. Another remarkable attraction is the park with its dragon's peak, museum of conservation and Nibelungenhalle memorial gallery.

Bad Honnef, the spa town at the foot of the Drachenfels, is another place that brings Germany's federal history to life: Bundeskanzler-Adenauer-Haus offers insights into the life of the first Chancellor, including his rose garden.

On the left bank of the river, just beyond the southern boundary of Bonn at Rolandseck, travellers will find an especially beautiful stretch of the Rhineland: amid the flow the islands of Nonnenwerth and Grafenwerth, on land the mid-19th century railway station that is synonymous with high culture on a small scale. The station – a work of art in itself – recently gained a spectacular extension in the form of the Arp Museum, built into the hillside behind. Suspended above is the Rolandsbogen archway – all that remains of Rolandseck castle and a beloved destination of romantics past and present.

Wahrzeichen der Rheinromantik: Der Rolandsbogen

A romantic landmark along the river Rhine: the Rolandsbogen

Kunst und Architektur vom Feinsten:
Das Arp-Museum in Rolandseck

Outstanding art and architecture:
the Arp Museum in Rolandseck

Gemächlich geht's mit der Fähre
über die Sieg

Ferry crossing the river Sieg at a
leisurely pace

Berühmter Rosengarten: Das Wohnhaus Konrad Adenauers

Famous rose garden: the residence of Konrad Adenauer

Vom Verkehr umbraust: Das Rhöndorfer Kapellchen

Surrounded by traffic: Rhöndorf chapel

Burgenromantik neben Nobelhotel: Drachenburg und Petersberg

Romantic castle meets luxury hotel: Drachenburg and Petersberg

Für Staatsgäste nur das Beste: Hotel Petersberg

Only the very best for state visitors: Hotel Petersberg

Bonn ganz international: UN Tower, World Conference Center, Deutsche Welle

Bonn goes international: UN Tower, World Conference Centre, Deutsche Welle

Beethoven und Schumann

Der Komponist ist in Bonn allgegenwärtig: Beethoven-Haus, Beethoven-Denkmal auf dem Münsterplatz, Beethovenhalle, Beethoven Competition, Beethoven-Stiftung, Beethoven-Festspiele ... Und seine Mutter liegt auf dem Alten Friedhof begraben, einer grünen, melancholischen Oase am Rande der Innenstadt, auf der zahlreiche Gelehrte und Prominente aller Couleur ihre letzte Ruhestätte haben. Dort fasziniert auch das Grabmal von Clara und Robert Schumann. Der Komponist hatte seine letzten Lebensjahre in der Irrenanstalt in Endenich verbracht. Er wird alljährlich mit den Schumannfest geehrt. Bonn ist übrigens die einzige Stadt, die jedes Jahr einen Stadtklangkünstler kürt. Kann man sein musikalisches Erbe phantasievoller würdigen?

Beethoven and Schumann

The composer is ever-present in Bonn, thanks to Beethoven-Haus, Beethoven Monument on Münsterplatz and Beethovenhalle, as well as the Beethoven Competition, Beethoven Foundation and Beethoven Festival. His mother is also buried in the Alter Friedhof cemetery, a reflective green space just outside the city centre where numerous scholars and prominent people from all walks of life are laid to rest. The tomb of Clara and Robert Schumann is intriguing. The composer, who spent the final years of his life in an asylum for the insane in Endenich, is honoured by an annual Schumannfest. Incidentally, Bonn is the only city to elect its own sound artist every year. Could there be a more imaginative tribute to its musical heritage?

In diesem Hinterhaus wurde Ludwig van Beethoven geboren

The birthplace of Ludwig van Beethoven

Auf dem Podest: Ludwig van Beethoven auf dem Münsterplatz

Memorial of Ludwig van Beethoven in Münsterplatz

Architektonisches Schmuckstück für Hörgenüsse der Extraklasse: Kammermusiksaal im Beethovenhaus

Exquisite music presented in an architectural jewel: chamber music hall in Beethovenhaus

Mit strengem Blick: Beethovendenkmal auf dem Münsterplatz

Casting a stern look: Beethoven memorial in Münsterplatz

Faszinierend für Groß und Klein: Beethovens Geburtshaus und sein Garten

Fascinating for young and old alike: Beethoven's birthplace and adjacent garden

Das Grabmal Robert und Clara Schumanns auf dem Alten Friedhof

Tomb of Robert and Clara Schumann in the Alter Friedhof

Made in Bonn

Wer kennt sie nicht, die Goldbären, Lakritzschnecken und Schaumgummi-Naschereien von Haribo? Sie sind buchstäblich weltweit in aller Munde. Aber nicht jeder weiß, dass sie aus Bonn kommen, obwohl sie die Stadt im Namen tragen: **Ha**ns **Ri**egel **Bo**nn ist der Erfinder, die Firma produziert noch heute am Rhein. Auch „ei, ei, ei Verpoorten" gehört zu den Bonner Markenzeichen. Über eine Million Eier verwandelt das Unternehmen täglich in den beliebten Likör. Überall in der Welt begegnet man auch den Orgeln aus dem Hause Klais, ob auf den Philippinen oder in den USA, in Litauen oder Spanien.

Made in Bonn

Everybody knows the golden bears, liquorice wheels and foam sweets of Haribo: around the world they are on everyone's lips, quite literally. However, not everyone is aware they are made in Bonn, even though the city appears in the brand name: they were invented by **Ha**ns **Ri**egel **Bo**nn, whose company continues to produce confectionery at its local site. Another Bonn brand is Verpoorten, which turns over a million eggs into a popular egg liqueur every day. Organs made by Klais are also exported all over the world: to the Philippines, the USA, Lithuania and Spain.

Orgeln von Klais erklingen in aller Welt

Organs built by Klais are renowned around the world

Zauberhafte Einheit: Bonn, der Rhein und das Siebengebirge

Enchanting unity: Bonn, the river Rhine and the Siebengebirge

Museen, Museen

Publikumsmagnet ist zweifellos die Museumsmeile mit Museum Alexander Koenig, Haus der Geschichte, Kunstmuseum Bonn und Kunst- und Ausstellungshalle der Bundesrepublik Deutschland. Auch das Deutsche Museum, die Bonner Dependance des Münchner Hauses, zählt sich dazu. Auch sonst ist die Bonner Museumslandschaft vielfältig: Stadtmuseum und Macke-Haus, Frauenmuseum und Arithmeum mit seinen Rechenmaschinen, LVR-Landesmuseum mit dem Schädel des Neandertalers, Ägyptisches Museum, Schumannhaus ...

Museums galore

There is no doubt that the Museum Mile – featuring the Museum Koenig, Haus der Geschichte, Kunstmuseum Bonn and the Art and Exhibition Hall of the Federal Republic of Germany – is a magnet to visitors. The diversity of Bonn's museums doesn't end there, though: the Deutsches Museum, the Bonn annexe of the Munich institution, can be added to the list along with the StadtMuseum, the August Macke Haus, the Women's Museum, the Arithmeum with its calculating machines, the LVR-Landes-Museum with its Neanderthal skull, the Egyptian Museum, the Schumannhaus and more.

Neugier auf Wissenschaft stillt das Deutsche Museum Bonn

Questions on scientific subjects are answered at the Deutsches Museum Bonn

Rechnen einst und jetzt: Das Arithmeum

Mathematics past and present: the Arithmeum

Unter Göttern: Die Abgusssammlung im Akademischen Kunstmuseum

Among gods: collection of casts at the Academic Museum of Art

Klassische Kunst in klassizistischer Umgebung: Das Akademische Kunstmuseum

Classical art in classical surroundings: the Academic Museum of Art

Archäologie, Kunst, Kulturgeschichte: Im LVR-Landesmuseum ist der Neandertaler zuhause

Archaeology, art, cultural history: the Neanderthal man has found a home at the LVR-Landesmuseum